TOOLS OF THE TRADE

SandCastle
Tools of the Trade

HAMMERS

ANDERS HANSON

Consulting Editor, Diane Craig, M.A./Reading Specialist

ABDO
Publishing Company

Published by ABDO Publishing Company, 8000 West 78th Street, Edina, Minnesota 55439.

Copyright © 2010 by Abdo Consulting Group, Inc. International copyrights reserved in all countries.

No part of this book may be reproduced in any form without written permission from the publisher. SandCastle™ is a trademark and logo of ABDO Publishing Company.

Printed in the United States.

Editor: Pam Price
Content Developer: Nancy Tuminelly
Cover and Interior Design and Production: Mighty Media
Photo Credits: Shutterstock, iStockphoto (Mark Bond, Stephen Shockley, Bernd Strasser), JupiterImages Corporation, Franklin D. Roosevelt Presidential Library and Museum

Library of Congress Cataloging-in-Publication Data
Hanson, Anders, 1980-
   Hammers / Anders Hanson.
      p. cm. -- (Tools of the trade)
   ISBN 978-1-60453-582-2
   1. Hammers--Juvenile literature. I. Title.

TJ1201.H3H35 2009
621.9'73--dc22
                              2008055052

SandCastle™ Level: Fluent

SandCastle™ books are created by a team of professional educators, reading specialists, and content developers around five essential components–phonemic awareness, phonics, vocabulary, text comprehension, and fluency–to assist young readers as they develop reading skills and strategies and increase their general knowledge. All books are written, reviewed, and leveled for guided reading, early reading intervention, and Accelerated Reader® programs for use in shared, guided, and independent reading and writing activities to support a balanced approach to literacy instruction. The SandCastle™ series has four levels that correspond to early literacy development. The levels are provided to help teachers and parents select appropriate books for young readers.

Emerging Readers
(no flags)

Beginning Readers
(1 flag)

Transitional Readers
(2 flags)

Fluent Readers
(3 flags)

SandCastle™ would like to hear from you. Please send us your comments and suggestions.

CONTENTS

What Is a Hammer?　4

History　5

Claw Hammer　**6**

Mallet　**10**

Sledgehammer　**14**

Jackhammer　**18**

Match Game　22

Tool Quiz　23

Glossary　24

sledgehammer

WHAT IS A HAMMER?

A hammer is a striking tool. Handheld hammers have a handle and a head. Powered hammers use **compressed** air to move the head up and down.

HISTORY

Scientists believe that humans began using simple tools more than two million years ago. The first tool was probably a hard rock held in the hand.

About 28,000 years ago, people attached wooden handles to rocks. The handles made the tools easier to use.

About 5,000 years ago, people learned to make hammer heads out of metal. They used metals such as bronze and copper.

ancient hammer

Today, hammer heads are usually made from steel.

CLAW HAMMER

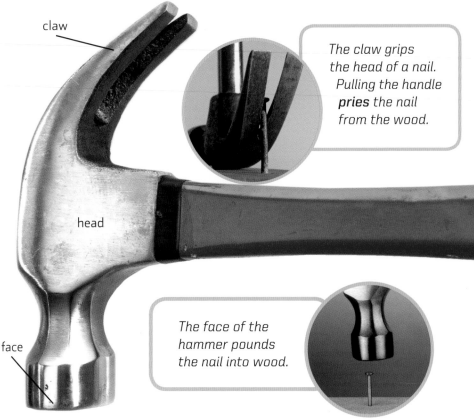

claw

The claw grips the head of a nail. Pulling the handle **pries** the nail from the wood.

head

face

The face of the hammer pounds the nail into wood.

6

handle

Claw hammers are used to pound and **pry** nails.

Pat repairs houses. He uses a claw hammer to fix a window.

Dan pounds a nail with a claw hammer.
He is working on the frame of a house.

MALLET

face

head

face

A mallet head has two faces. The faces are larger than the face on a claw hammer.

*Mallets are used often in **carpentry** and construction. They are also used in sports such as croquet.*

wooden mallet

handle

Unlike most hammers, mallets have soft heads.

Mallet heads are usually made of **materials** such as rubber or wood. The soft heads are less likely to damage objects or surfaces than steel heads are.

Edward is putting tile in his basement.
He uses a mallet to level the tiles.

Ethan is making a door.
He strikes a **chisel** with a mallet.

handle

Sledgehammers have long handles and heavy heads.

Some sledgehammers weigh as much as 20 pounds (9 kg). Because they are so heavy, they can hit things harder than lighter hammers can.

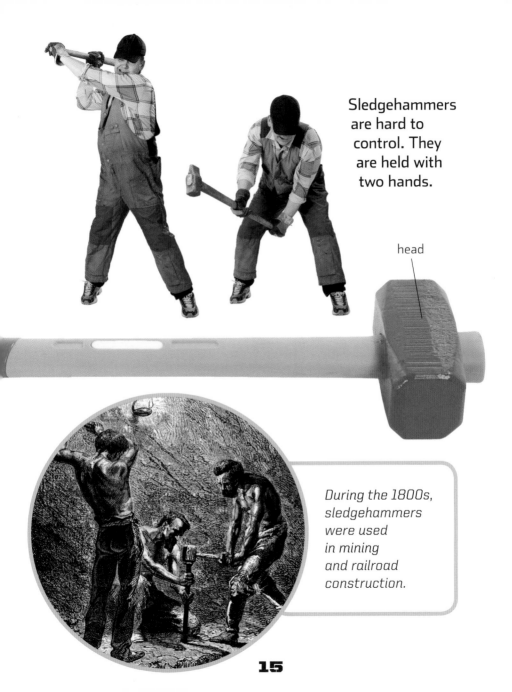

Sledgehammers are hard to control. They are held with two hands.

head

During the 1800s, sledgehammers were used in mining and railroad construction.

Ray is a construction worker.
He **drives** stakes with a sledgehammer.

Bud is tearing down a building. He uses a sledgehammer to break concrete.

JACKHAMMER

A jackhammer has a bit instead of a head. The bit moves up and down. It can break up hard **materials** such as concrete.

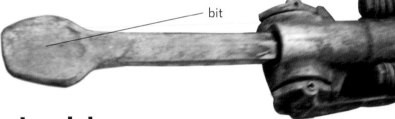

bit

Jackhammers are powered by **compressed** air.

A hose connects the jackhammer to an air compressor. The compressor forces air through the hose and into the jackhammer. The air moves the bit up and down.

handle

Jackhammers **vibrate**
and make lots of noise.
It takes two hands to
hold a jackhammer.

handle

Eddy is working on a **foundation**.
He is holding a jackhammer.

Johnny is using a jackhammer.
He is breaking up a concrete curb.

MATCH GAME

Match the words to the pictures! The answers are on the bottom of the page.

1. jackhammer

A.

2. mallet

B.

3. sledgehammer

C.

4. claw hammer

D.

TOOL QUIZ

Test your tool knowledge with this quiz!
The answers are on the bottom of the page.

1. Claw hammers are used to pry nails from wood. True or false?

2. Mallet heads are usually made from steel. True or false?

3. Sledgehammers have light heads. True or false?

4. Jackhammers are powered by compressed air. True or false?

GLOSSARY

carpentry – the job of making or fixing wooden things.

chisel – a tool with a sharp metal wedge and a handle.

compress – to squeeze or press into a small area.

drive – to use physical force to make something move forward.

foundation – the base for something.

material – the substance something is made of, such as metal, fabric, or plastic.

pry – to move, raise, or pull apart using force.

vibrate – to move back and forth rapidly.

To see a complete list of SandCastle™ books and other nonfiction titles from ABDO Publishing Company, visit www.abdopublishing.com.

8000 West 78th Street, Edina, MN 55439 • 800-800-1312 • fax 952-831-1632